A LifeBuilder Bible Study

IMAGES
of CHRIST

10 studies
for individuals or groups

Dale & Sandy Larsen

With Notes for Leaders

Scripture Union is an international Christian charity working with churches in more than 130 countries.

Thank you for purchasing this book. Any profits from this book support SU in England and Wales to bring the good news of Jesus Christ to children, young people and families and to enable them to meet God through the Bible and prayer.

Find out more about our work and how you can get involved at:

www.scriptureunion.org.uk (England and Wales)
www.suscotland.org.uk (Scotland)
www.suni.co.uk (Northern Ireland)
www.scriptureunion.org (USA)
www.su.org.au (Australia)

ISBN 978 1 84427 248 8

First published in the United States by InterVarsity Press 2006.
© Dale & Sandy Larsen

This edition published in the United Kingdom © Scripture Union 2007, reprinted 2010, 2016.

Scripture quotations, unless otherwise indicated, are taken from the Holy Bible, New International Version. Copyright © 1973, 1978, 1984 by International Bible Society. Anglicisation copyright © 1979, 1984, 1989. Used by permission of Hodder and Stoughton Limited.

British Library Cataloguing-in-Publication data: a catalogue record for this book is available from the British Library.

Printed in Malta by Gutenberg Press Ltd.

Contents

Getting the Most Out of
Images of Christ

What do you picture in your mind when you think of Jesus Christ?

While we can't predict your answer, chances are good that you think of Jesus as the good shepherd, bearing a lamb on his shoulders. You may have such a picture in your church or your home. There may even be one in your Bible.

But why would an artist portray Jesus as a shepherd? David was a shepherd before he became king of Israel, but Jesus was a carpenter before he began his ministry. We have the image of Jesus as shepherd for a very good reason: he called himself the good shepherd. He invited us to think of him that way.

Jesus used other word-pictures for himself, such as the light of the world, the bread of life and the true vine. Those images do not spring to our minds as readily as the good shepherd because they are not personal, but the Lord freely applied them to himself.

From Old Testament prophecy come other images of the Messiah: the suffering servant, the branch, the cornerstone. John the Baptist identified Jesus as the Lamb of God. The apostle Paul portrayed him as the divine bridegroom (as did John in the book of Revelation) and as the head of the body, the church. The apostle Peter developed the prophecy of Christ as the cornerstone for a temple of living stones.

As we study each scriptural image of Christ, we want to

focus on *our relationship to the reality behind the image*. The good shepherd remains only a sentimental picture if we do not follow him. The light of the world does not help us if we choose to remain in darkness. Christ is our cornerstone, but only if we allow ourselves to be built into his house.

At the conclusion of each study, you will find three extra features:

- guidance for prayer. Feel free to use the ideas for prayer whether you are studying in a group or individually.

- a "Now or Later" section. Here you will find suggestions for further study and ways to confirm the lesson and apply it to everyday life.

- a list of hymns based on the scriptural image. Many hymns have been inspired by the rich poetic imagery of the Bible. Sing one or more of them, or simply read the words. If some are unfamiliar to your group, use the opportunity to learn the songs and reclaim some of the rich heritage of hymns based on scriptural language. You will probably recall other hymns or choruses based on each image.

May these studies bring you closer to Christ through the pictures that the Bible paints in words.

Suggestions for Individual Study

1. As you begin each study, pray that God will speak to you through his Word.

2. Read the introduction to the study and respond to the personal reflection question or exercise. This is designed to help you focus on God and on the theme of the study.

3. Each study deals with a particular passage—so that you can delve into the author's meaning in that context. Read and reread the passage to be studied. The questions are written using the language of the New International Version, so you may wish to use that version of the Bible. The New Revised Standard Version is also recommended.

4. This is an inductive Bible study, designed to help you discover for yourself what Scripture is saying. The study includes three types of questions. *Observation* questions ask about the basic facts: who, what, when, where and how. *Interpretation* questions delve into the meaning of the passage. *Application* questions help you discover the implications of the text for growing in Christ. These three keys unlock the treasures of Scripture.

Write your answers to the questions in the spaces provided or in a personal journal. Writing can bring clarity and deeper understanding of yourself and of God's Word.

5. It might be good to have a Bible dictionary handy. Use it to look up any unfamiliar words, names or places.

6. Use the prayer suggestion to guide you in thanking God for what you have learned and to pray about the applications that have come to mind.

7. You may want to go on to the suggestion under "Now or Later," or you may want to use that idea for your next study.

Suggestions for Members of a Group Study

1. Come to the study prepared. Follow the suggestions for individual study mentioned above. You will find that careful preparation will greatly enrich your time spent in group discussion.

2. Be willing to participate in the discussion. The leader of your group will not be lecturing. Instead, he or she will be encouraging the members of the group to discuss what they have learned. The leader will be asking the questions that are found in this guide.

3. Stick to the topic being discussed. Your answers should be based on the verses which are the focus of the discussion and not on outside authorities such as commentaries or speakers. These studies focus on a particular passage of Scripture. Only rarely should you refer to other portions of the Bible. This allows for everyone to participate in in-depth study on equal ground.

4. Be sensitive to the other members of the group. Listen attentively when they describe what they have learned. You may be surprised by their insights! Each question assumes a variety of answers. Many questions do not have "right" answers, particularly questions that aim at meaning or application. Instead the questions push us to explore the passage more thoroughly.

When possible, link what you say to the comments of others. Also, be affirming whenever you can. This will encourage some of the more hesitant members of the group to participate.

5. Be careful not to dominate the discussion. We are sometimes so eager to express our thoughts that we leave too little opportunity for others to respond. By all means participate! But allow others to also.

6. Expect God to teach you through the passage being discussed and through the other members of the group. Pray that you will have an enjoyable and profitable time together, but also that as a result of the study you will find ways that you can take action individually and/or as a group.

7. Remember that anything said in the group is considered confidential and should not be discussed outside the group unless specific permission is given to do so.

8. If you are the group leader, you will find additional suggestions at the back of the guide.

1

Good Shepherd

John 10:1-18

Our culture puts a high value on independence. The self-made man or woman wins far more respect than one who inherits a fortune or who rises to the top through family connections. Everyone wants to be seen as self-reliant and self-sufficient. Dependence is weakness; independence is strength.

If we are honest, however, there are times when we get tired of running our own lives and would gladly hand over control to someone else.

GROUP DISCUSSION. In what areas of life is it good to be dependent, and why? Use examples from your own experience as well as what you have observed in other people's lives.

PERSONAL REFLECTION. When you think of letting someone else take care of you, how do you respond?

The Jewish religious leaders were becoming increasingly hostile toward Jesus. They called him demon-possessed and tried to stone him for blasphemy. In such an atmosphere of conflict,

Jesus drew a word-picture of himself that still brings peace and comfort to his followers. *Read John 10:1-18.*

1. In what ways is the good shepherd different from all others who might show an interest in the sheep?

2. Suppose you stood in the crowd and heard Jesus say all this. Do you think you would immediately want to be one of the "sheep," or would you have reservations? Why or why not?

3. Why do the sheep trust the shepherd and mistrust the stranger (vv. 1-5)?

4. Imagine that you are a sheep in that sheep pen and the events of verses 3-4 take place. What do you see, hear and feel?

5. Because his hearers do not fully understand him (v. 6), Jesus changes his metaphor for himself in verses 7-10. What is the significance of the fact that Christ calls himself *both* the gate for the sheepfold and the shepherd who leads his sheep through the gate?

6. How have you found that Christ gives "life . . . to the full" (v. 10, "more abundantly" KJV)?

---

7. In verses 11-18, Jesus returns to identifying himself as the shepherd, and more specifically as the "good shepherd" (vv. 11, 14). To what lengths will the good shepherd go in order to save the lives of his sheep, and why (vv. 11-13)?

---

8. What are some "wolves" that threaten the church (all Christians) both internally and externally?

---

9. How do verses 14-18 add to the picture of Jesus as the shepherd?

---

10. As you consider the relationship of the shepherd and the sheep, what are the responsibilities of the sheep? Consider both their actions and their attitudes.

11. When have you been especially grateful to have a Good Shepherd?

12. In what parts of your life do you need to follow the Shepherd more closely or more willingly?

Make Psalm 23 your prayer. As you pray, put your trust in the Good Shepherd. Thank him that he did not run away but willingly laid down his life for you.

Now or Later

- Because Scripture contains so many references to shepherds and sheep, your possibilities for further study are almost endless. A major Old Testament reference is Ezekiel 34, and of course there is Psalm 23. Some further New Testament references are Hebrews 13:20-21 and 1 Peter 2:21-25 and 5:1-4.
- Using Bible reference books, do further study about biblical shepherds and sheep.
- Jesus said that his sheep follow him because they know him (vv. 4, 14). No doubt you know someone who has been taken in by a false religious teacher; perhaps it has happened to you. Discuss ways you can learn to recognize the voice of Jesus so you are not deceived by false teachers.

Suggested hymns to read or sing
The Lord's My Shepherd, I'll Not Want; The King of Love My Shepherd Is; O Though In Whose Presence My Soul Takes Delight; In Heavenly Love Abiding; Savior, Like a Shepherd Lead Us; He Leadeth Me, O Blessed Thought

2

Lamb of God

A friend of ours donated one of her kidneys to a relative who desperately needed a kidney transplant. As usual in a small town, many people felt free to voice their opinions of her sacrifice. Why should she put her own health at risk and put her husband and children through such trauma, especially with no guarantee that her kidney would save her relative's life? On the other hand, how could she refuse to sacrifice her kidney when she was the best available match and she might save her relative's life? A person who makes a sacrifice declares the worth of the one for whom the sacrifice was made. Christ the Lamb of God sacrificed himself for us because he considered us worth the sacrifice.

GROUP DISCUSSION. What makes a great sacrifice worth it? Provide examples from your own experience.

PERSONAL REFLECTION. When have you sacrificed something very important for someone else? What made the person worth the sacrifice?

In Revelation 5:1-5, the apostle John has a vision of God on a throne, holding a scroll sealed with seven seals. John is grieved because there is no one worthy to break the seals. Then he hears that "the Lion of the tribe of Judah, the Root of David"— a reference to Christ—has triumphed and is worthy to open the scroll. *Read Revelation 5:6-14.*

---

1. Christ has just been identified as the "Lion of Judah" who is worthy to open the scroll (v. 5). In view of that majestic title, what is surprising and unusual about the appearance of the Lamb?

---

2. From verses 6-7 what do you learn about the Lamb's character and accomplishments?

---

3. After the Lamb takes the scroll, three groups in heaven sing joyfully in response (vv. 8-13). What more do we find out about the Lamb from their three songs?

---

4. Which phrases in the songs do you respond to most strongly, and why?

5. From verses 9-10, what do we learn about the people Christ purchased by his death?

---

6. How does the response of this multitude of worshipers compare with worship services in which you have participated?

---

7. It is easy to find comfort in the image of Jesus as the innocent, gentle Lamb of God. How does this passage challenge such a view?

---

8. How are the death of the Lamb and the triumph of the Lamb tied together?

---

9. When we think of offering worship, we often picture someone who is "high and exalted" (as in Isaiah 6:1) like a royal personage on an unapproachable throne. What is it about this Lamb that demands such a worshipful response?

10. John's Gospel records that John the Baptist called Jesus "the Lamb of God, who takes away the sin of the world" (John 1:29). How will a person's view of the seriousness of sin affect his or her response to Christ as the Lamb of God?

11. In what areas of your life do you take sin too casually?

12. What steps will you take to remind yourself that your sins required the death of Christ, the Lamb of God?

Offer praise to the Lamb of God in the words of Revelation 5:12 or in your own words. Thank him for willingly giving his life for you.

Now or Later

- Study God's instructions for the first Passover in Exodus 12:1-30 and Peter's interpretation of Christ in 1 Peter 1:17-21.
- Listen to the chorus "Worthy is the Lamb," which comes just before the final "Amen" in Handel's *Messiah*. Feel free to sing along!

Suggested hymns to read or sing
Crown Him with Many Crowns; Hail, Thou Once Despised Jesus; Thine Be the Glory, Risen Conquering Son; Ten Thousand Times Ten Thousand; Arise, My Soul, Arise

3

Suffering Servant

Isaiah 52:13—53:6

You can judge the age of a play or movie by whether the cast of characters includes a maid and/or a butler. Butlers and maids are stock characters of movies and stage plays, but only before a certain point in history. Now modern appliances and gadgets have replaced servants. Even the word *servant* sounds outmoded. An employer would never refer to an employee as *my servant*; the title would be considered demeaning. We might like to be commended for our *service* to our church, community or business, but we would dislike being called a *servant*.

GROUP DISCUSSION. When has someone been a servant to you, not for pay but out of love? How did you feel about being served?

PERSONAL REFLECTION. When have you willingly acted as a servant for someone else? What motivated you to serve?

In the book of Acts, Philip overhears an Ethiopian official reading from the book of Isaiah. The passage speaks of someone who was like a lamb led to slaughter or a sheep before its shearers. The Ethiopian asks Philip who the prophet meant, and

Philip explains that the passage is about Jesus Christ (Acts 8:26-35). *Read Isaiah 52:13—53:6,* which leads up to the passage read by the Ethiopian.

---

1. This passage begins with a promise (52:13). How does the rest of the passage appear to contradict the promise?

---

2. If you met the servant as Isaiah describes him here, how do you think you would react?

---

3. What will be the servant's impact on the people who encounter him (52:14-15)? (For "sprinkle" in 52:15, an alternative translation is "startle.")

---

4. How would you characterize the servant's beginnings (53:1-2)?

---

5. Why do people find the servant repellent (53:2-3)?

6. According to 53:4-6, what are God's purposes in the suffering of the servant?

7. How are God's purposes misunderstood (53:4)?

8. What part does God's justice play in the servant's sufferings (53:5)?

9. How does humanity benefit from the faithful obedience of the servant (53:4-6)?

10. In the preceding study you saw the crowds in heaven praising the victorious Lamb of God. Isaiah 53 shows the pain that preceded the victory. How do both together add to your understanding of Jesus?

11. Verse 6 tells us two great truths: we have all strayed, and the Lord has put our sins onto his servant. How have you experienced the reality of both parts of verse 6?

---

12. Where do you still struggle to believe that Christ has taken on the guilt of *all* your sin?

---

13. What reassurance of forgiveness do you gain from this Scripture?

Pray for grateful hearts that will thank the Servant for all he has done for you. Thank him that he did not quit with his work half done but completed it for our salvation.

Now or Later

- Continue your study of the suffering servant in Isaiah 53:7-12, which takes the servant's suffering all the way to death and then to exaltation by God.
- Study Philippians 2:5-11, Paul's hymn to the servanthood and exaltation of Jesus.
- Study 1 Peter 2:18-25, in which Peter urges his readers to imitate Christ's example of patience and faith in suffering.

Suggested hymns to read or sing

Make Me a Servant; Man of Sorrows, What a Name; O Sacred Head, Now Wounded; Thou Didst Leave Thy Throne

4

Branch

The American chestnut was a massive tree that could reach a height of 100 feet. We say "was" because in 1904, beginning in New York, a fungal disease called chestnut blight began to kill off the trees. Within forty years most chestnut trees in the eastern United States were gone. But below ground, the roots of some trees survived the chestnut blight. Alongside dead stumps, the living roots put out shoots, which began to grow into trees. Today there are American chestnut trees twenty feet tall. Given a few more decades, they will achieve the height of their 100-foot ancestors—a testimony to life and the toughness of trees.

GROUP DISCUSSION. Recall a time you swung on a tire swing or some other kind of swing suspended from a tree branch. What qualities did the branch need in order to support you safely and give you a good ride?

PERSONAL REFLECTION. When has God brought about changes in your life that were beyond anything you had wished or prayed for?

Isaiah described the coming Messiah as a shoot who would arise from the stump of Jesse and who would develop into a fruit-bearing *branch*. Isaiah did not make a random word choice. Christ is not only a branch from David's lineage; he will bear a new kind of fruit among humanity. King David's father was Jesse of Bethlehem (1 Samuel 16). God promised Israel that a descendant of David would rule over them forever (see Psalm 132:11-12). When Jesus entered Jerusalem, the crowds hailed him as the "Son of David" (Matthew 21:9). *Read Isaiah 11:1-9.*

---

1. What revolutionary changes will the Branch bring about?

---

2. What aspect of the reign of the Branch speaks to you most deeply, and why?

---

3. How is the Branch related to Jesse (and therefore to David, v. 1)?

---

4. In what ways will the Branch have a special relationship with the Spirit of God (v. 2)?

5. How will the character of the Branch be different from that of any other earthly ruler (vv. 2-5)?

6. Make a sketch or chart of the extraordinary pairings in verses 6-8. What do the images have in common?

7. In one word or one phrase, how would you describe the world portrayed in verses 6-8?

8. How are the end of injury and the knowledge of the Lord connected (v. 9)?

9. Looking back over this passage, what is it about the reign of the Branch that will bring harmony to the world?

10. How has Christ brought a foretaste of this peace and harmony to you?

---

11. Where do you especially need counsel from the One who has the Spirit of wisdom and understanding, counsel and power, knowledge and fear of the Lord (v. 2)?

Pray for the peace of Christ in the world, in your community, in your church, in your family and in yourself.

Now or Later

Study other references to the Branch in Isaiah 4:2-6 and Jeremiah 23:5-6; 33:14-22.

Suggested hymns to read or sing

Lo, How a Rose E'er Blooming; O Come, O Come, Emmanuel

5

True Vine

John 15:1-8

One area of our local city park was thick with wild blackberry bushes. We picked gallons of them and made jam (yes, picking wild fruit is legal on public land). A few weeks ago, we were shocked to see that the blackberry bushes had been chopped off. The long thorny branches from which we hoped to pick more berries this summer are now stacks of dead brush. Apparently some park employee saw the berry bushes as nothing but nuisance undergrowth. We can only hope that new shoots will come up from the stubs that are left, because there is no hope for the branches. They have been cut off from their source of life.

GROUP DISCUSSION. From what sources do you draw strength? How would your life be different if you were cut off from them?

PERSONAL REFLECTION. How has the Lord pruned away things in your life that were not spiritually profitable? How did you respond to the pruning process?

The imagery of Christ in Scripture takes some surprising turns. For example, Jesus is both Good Shepherd and Lamb of God. After his designation as Branch in the prophecies of Isaiah and Jeremiah, he calls believers "branches" of himself in the Gospel of John. At their last Passover meal together, Jesus engages in a long conversation with his disciples. The Gospel writers Matthew, Mark and Luke tell us a little of what is said, but John reveals much more. *Read John 15:1-8.*

1. What is the relationship of the gardener, the vine and the branches?

2. What is your emotional reaction to these words of Jesus?

3. How are the branches dependent on the vine?

4. Jesus called himself the "true vine" (v. 1). What are some false "vines" from which people try to draw energy and purpose?

5. How will the gardener (God the Father) use his pruning knife differently on the fruitful and the unfruitful branches (vv. 1-2)?

6. How would you describe a fruitful Christian life?

7. What do you think makes the difference between a fruitful and an unfruitful Christian life?

8. How would you explain what it means to "remain in" Christ (vv. 4-7)?

9. Who or what has helped and encouraged you to remain in Christ?

10. Many people who make no claim to be Christians have accomplished great things. How do you justify Jesus' absolute assertion that "apart from me you can do nothing" (v. 5)?

11. What are some warning signs that Christians are trying to bear fruit without depending on Christ?

12. The second half of verse 7 appears to be a guarantee that God will give us anything we ask. What are the implications of the "if" clause at the beginning of the sentence?

13. What steps will you take to continue your dependence on Christ as the source of life and fruitfulness?

Thank the Lord for joining you to himself in salvation. Thank him for his life-giving and life-sustaining power. Pray that he will keep you faithful and dependent on him for everything.

Now or Later
Study 1 John 2:24-28, in which John expresses the hope that his readers will remain in Christ and that the truth of Christ will remain in them.

Suggested hymns to read or sing
I Need Thee Every Hour; O Jesus, I Have Promised

6

Light of the World

John 1:1-9

A Venezuelan student told us that when he was very young, his father would lead him into completely dark rooms and make him walk through them alone. The father's purpose was to teach the child not to be afraid of the dark. The student now says that he has no fear of walking in even total darkness.

Most of us were not trained like our Venezuelan friend. When the power fails and the lights suddenly go out, we are afraid or at least nervous. Imagination quickly replaces rationality. As we stumble around and search for a flashlight or matches, we listen for strange sounds, and we are afraid of what our fingers might touch.

People of Jesus' time had to rely on oil lamps and occasional moonlight for nighttime illumination. They must have had an especially keen appreciation for a light that could not be put out.

GROUP DISCUSSION. Recall a time when you were unexpectedly plunged into total darkness. What emotions did you go through? If you were afraid, how did you try to calm yourself? If you were not afraid, to what do you attribute your lack of fear?

PERSONAL REFLECTION. How does light affect your daily life physically and emotionally?

As John begins his Gospel, he uses symbolic language to introduce a person who made everything, can grant life and can make people into children of God. Not until verse 17 does John identify this person as Jesus Christ. *Read John 1:1-9.*

1. From this passage what do you know about the "light" that John wrote about?

2. When have you especially sensed the difference between the light of Christ and the darkness of the world?

3. How is the Word of verses 1-3 identified with God himself?

4. "Light" is first introduced in verses 4-5. What is remarkable about this light?

5. In verse 5, the Greek word translated *understood* can also be translated *overcome*. In what ways is Christ neither understood nor overcome by the powers of darkness?

6. What role did John the Baptist play in the coming of the light of Christ (vv. 6-9)?

7. Christ is identified as the "true light" (v. 9). How could a light be false?

8. Not everyone walks in the light of Christ. In what sense can Christ be said to give light to every person (v. 9)?

9. Write about a time that you came to see a situation or another person in the light of Christ. What difference did it make in your attitude?

10. In what areas of your life do you feel that darkness rather than light still dominates? Consider both areas of sin and areas of confusion.

11. How will you bring your life more fully into the light of Christ?

12. How will you enlist the help of others to bring your life into the light of Christ?

---

13. How do you see yourself bringing the light of Christ to others?

Thank the Lord that he has not left you in darkness. Pray that you will see others in his light.

Now or Later

- Study John 3:16-21; 8:12; and 12:34-36—the other places in John's Gospel where Jesus is identified with light.
- Study 1 John 1:5-7 and 2:7-11 for more words of the apostle John about the contrast of darkness and the light of Christ.

Suggested hymns to read or sing
When Morning Gilds the Skies; Christ Is the World's True Light; The Whole World Was Lost in the Darkness of Sin; Fairest Lord Jesus (also called *Beautiful Savior*); *Turn Your Eyes Upon Jesus*

7

Bridegroom

Ephesians 5:25-33

At most weddings it is the bride who shines. Although the entrance of the groom signals the beginning of the ceremony, he arrives without much fanfare. The entrance of the bride is dramatic, even spectacular. She is the one who dazzles the eye. The guests know that the bride and groom are equally important, but the arrangement of the ceremony makes it uniquely *her* day.

In Jesus' time and place, the groom was more central to the wedding ceremony. The bridegroom and his party left his home and proceeded to the bride's home, where she and her party were waiting. In a joyful procession the groom then escorted the bride back to his home, where the wedding took place and the festivities continued for several days, while the best man or "friend of the bridegroom" acted as master of ceremonies.

GROUP DISCUSSION. How does commitment to Christ resemble the commitment of a marriage partner to a spouse?

PERSONAL REFLECTION. When have you been especially aware of the love of Christ for you? When have you been especially aware of his cleansing forgiveness?

Christ is referred to as the Bridegroom in several places in Scripture, but the writers do not elaborate on the relationship of bride and bridegroom. In a well-known passage in his letter to the Ephesians, Paul expanded on the image of Christ as husband of his bride, the church. *Read Ephesians 5:25-33.*

1. Throughout this passage how is Christ portrayed as the ideal husband/bridegroom?

2. Whether you are a woman or a man, what are your feelings as you consider life with a marriage partner who has the qualities Paul describes here?

3. How does Christ show sacrificial love for his bride, the church (vv. 25-27, 29)?

4. How is the bride changed because of the bridegroom's sacrifice for her (vv. 26-27)?

5. Many people resist submitting to Christ as Lord because they fear it will restrict their freedom. How do verses 25-27 take submission to Christ out of the realm of just following rules?

6. How do verses 28-31 express the husband's intimacy with the wife?

7. How has your intimacy with Christ helped you in times of crisis?

8. Verse 31 offers the same instruction given to Adam and Eve in Genesis 2:24. How is the relationship between husband and wife similar to the relationship between Christ and the church?

9. Where do you struggle to trust your divine bridegroom's love and care for you?

10. How will you commit those areas of life to the Lord this week?

---

11. What will you do differently this week because you love the bridegroom, Jesus Christ?

As you pray, tell the Lord that you love him. Thank him that he loves you freely even though you can never deserve his love.

Now or Later

- Consider: In what ways is the church, the bride of Christ, tempted to outshine her divine bridegroom?
- Study other scriptural references to Christ as bridegroom: Matthew 25:1-13; Mark 2:18-20; John 3:22-30; Revelation 19:6-9.

Suggested hymns to read or sing
The Church's One Foundation; Rejoice, Rejoice, Believers; Immortal Love, Forever Full; My Jesus, I Love Thee; Jesus, Lover of My Soul

8

Head of the Church

Colossians 1:15-20

A mother said of her two teenagers, "They'd forget their heads if they weren't attached." Have you ever explained a thoughtless action by saying, "I lost my head" or "I don't know where my head was"? The statements cannot be literally true, because a person without a head can't do anything. A person can lose several major body parts and still live, but no person can live without a head.

Just as a headless body cannot be alive, the church is lifeless without Christ. The difference is not one of degree; it is absolute. The presence of Christ does not simply make the church stronger or more energetic. Without Christ, the church has no life at all.

GROUP DISCUSSION. What have you seen happen in churches when Christ is not at the center of what is going on?

PERSONAL REFLECTION. What difference would it make in your church if Christ were absent from all worship services, committee meetings, business meetings, social events and all other activities?

Christians in Colossae were being misled by false teachers who wanted to initiate converts into a secret mystical knowledge beyond the gospel. Paul wrote to remind the Colossians that Christ is all-sufficient, now and forever. *Read Colossians 1:15-20.* ("He" is Jesus Christ.)

---

1. What are the various uses of the word *all* in this passage?

---

2. Which use of the word *all* speaks to you most deeply, and why?

---

3. How is Christ involved in creating and sustaining the world (vv. 15-17)?

---

4. In what sense does a head have supremacy over the body to which it is attached?

---

5. In what sense does Christ have supremacy over the church (v. 18)?

6. How could all of God's fullness be said to dwell in the man Jesus (v. 19)?

7. What was Christ's great work of reconciliation (v. 20)?

8. Suppose someone said to you, "I need Christ for the religious or spiritual part of my life, but I have to be realistic about getting what I need in all the other parts of my life." Using Colossians 1:15-20, how would you respond to that claim?

9. In the everyday lives of Christians, what are some practical implications of the fact that Christ is head of the church?

10. To what other false "heads" does the body of Christ try to attach itself, and with what results?

11. Who or what else are you tempted to follow as supreme, other than Christ?

---

12. What will you do this week to set aside other "heads" and depend on Christ alone?

Yield every part of your life to Christ as you pray. Acknowledge him as your Head, your only source of life.

Now or Later

- Draw yourself with many heads. Label each head with something you follow or on which you rely, other than Jesus Christ. Cross out or erase each head and replace them with one head, that of Christ.
- Study 1 Corinthians 12:12-31, in which Paul develops the image of the church as the body of Christ.
- Study Ephesians 4:1-16, a passage about unity that concludes with the image of Christ as head of the body.

Suggested hymns to read or sing
Be Thou My Vision; Ask Ye What Great Thing I Know; Blessing and Honor and Glory and Power

9

Bread of Life

John 6:25-51

During our year in Ukraine we practically lived on dense dark Russian bread. I wanted to know how to make the bread so we could continue to enjoy it after we returned to the United States. A student wrote out instructions for me, but I have not often tried to bake the bread. I admit I am intimidated by a recipe that begins "16 kilograms flour, 8 liters water, 160 grams salt."

North Americans find it hard to think of bread as a necessity of life. Russians understand the concept, and so did the people of Jesus' time and place. When Jesus called himself the bread of life, he was not talking about the piece of toast that accompanies the breakfast egg or the bun that surrounds the hamburger. He meant that he was the difference between life and starvation.

GROUP DISCUSSION. What gives you life and keeps you going? How has your answer to that question changed in the past several years (if it has)?

PERSONAL REFLECTION. In times of crisis, who or what do you rely on most?

Who or what do you rely on most in everyday life? Why?

After Jesus miraculously fed over 5,000 people with five barley loaves and two fish, he went away by himself. When he
did not return by nightfall, his disciples started across the Sea
of Galilee to Capernaum without him. During the night he
walked on the water and joined them in the boat. The next
day, the crowds he had fed went looking for him and were
surprised to find him on the other side of the lake. *Read John
6:25-51.*

1. How is Jesus, the bread of life, similar to physical bread?

How is he different?

2. Jesus calls himself "the true bread from heaven" (v. 32), "the
bread of God" (v. 33), "the bread of life" (vv. 35, 48) and "the
living bread" (v. 51)? What comes to your mind when you read
his claims?

3. How did Jesus caution the people who sought him out (vv.
25-29)?

4. Everyone requires physical food in order to live. Most people must work to earn it. Knowing this, how would you account for Jesus' admonition *not* to work for the food that spoils but for the food that endures to eternal life (v. 27)?

5. How did the crowd show their dissatisfaction with Jesus' answers (vv. 30-34)?

6. As the bread of life, what does Jesus promise his followers (vv. 35-40)?

7. What relationship does Jesus assert to have with the Father (vv. 37-40)?

8. In verses 35-40, Jesus calls himself the bread of life (v. 35) but then he appears to change the subject. How do the rest of his words still fit with the idea that he is the one who gives and sustains life?

9. How is Jesus different from the manna in the desert (vv. 41-51)?

10. In what ways do you think you expend yourself for "the food that spoils" rather than feeding on Christ?

---

11. How does a Christian feed on the bread of life?

---

12. What will you do to remind yourself that you must rely on Christ not only for guidance or peace or temporal needs, but for *everything?*

Speak or write prayers of trust in the Lord. Thank him that he gives you life and sustains you. Commit each area of your life to him with a conscious decision that you will rely on him for everything.

Now or Later

- Discuss this question: What difference would it make if Jesus had said, "I give you the bread of life" rather than "I am the bread of life"?
- Study the story of the manna in the desert in Exodus 16.
- Study Paul's instructions for the Lord's Supper in 1 Corinthians 11:23-34.

Suggested hymns to read or sing
Break Thou the Bread of Life; Jesus, Thou Joy of Loving Hearts; All to Jesus I Surrender

10

Cornerstone

1 Peter 2:4-8

If you have been part of a church that built a new building, no doubt you remember a special service at which church members laid the building's cornerstone. What is called the laying of a church's cornerstone is usually a ceremonial act that takes place *after* the building is completed. A shallow stone facing is set into the real cornerstone of the building. If the real cornerstone were not already in place, the building could not stand.

GROUP DISCUSSION. Compare the foundation of a building to the foundation of a person's life. Why is the foundation of a life important?

PERSONAL REFLECTION. Consider this statement: "I know that the foundation of my life can never be shaken." Do you agree or disagree, and why?

As the physical cornerstone is essential to the structure of the church building, Jesus Christ is essential to the life of his people. The church *begins* with Christ and cannot be built without him. The apostle Peter wrote his first letter to Christians who had been scattered by persecution. Originally named Simon, he was given the name Peter (rock) by Jesus. In this letter Peter draws on Old Testament images of stones, which Jesus had used in his teaching. *Read 1 Peter 2:4-8.*

1. Who are the plural *stones* and the singular *stone* in this passage?

2. *Stones* sound like lifeless things. How do you respond to the idea that you are part of a spiritual house made up of living stones?

3. How is God's spiritual house built, according to verses 4-6?

4. What are the privileges and responsibilities of those who are built on Christ as cornerstone (vv. 5-6)?

5. In what sense will those who trust in Christ "never be put to shame" (v. 6)?

6. When those who are in rebellion against God encounter the cornerstone, what happens (vv. 7-8)?

7. At some point in your life did you stumble over this stone (Christ)? If so, what changed your mind about him?

8. Peter wrote that Christ is the cornerstone of the church as a whole, but he also spoke of *living stones*, individual Christians (v. 5). On what other cornerstone or cornerstones do you try to build your life?

9. What would be different for you if Christ were your sole cornerstone?

10. What changes would you like to make to tear down false foundations and allow Christ to build your life?

As you pray, express confidence in Christ your sure foundation. Ask him to show you any false security you have built up, and invite him to continue to build your life as he sees fit.

Now or Later

- First Peter 2:4-8 includes quotes from three Old Testament passages: Isaiah 28:16, Psalm 118:22 and Isaiah 8:14. Read and study them in context.

- Jesus left no doubt that Psalm 118:22-23 applied to him when he quoted the words in a dispute with religious leaders in Jerusalem (Mark 12:1-12). Later, Peter quoted from the passage when he and John were brought before the religious authorities, perhaps some of the same people (Acts 4:1-11). Study both passages.

- Paul also wrote of the church as the building of God with Christ as cornerstone. Study his words in Ephesians 2:19-22.

Suggested hymns to read or sing
Christ Is Made the Sure Foundation; The Church's One Foundation; Glorious Things of Thee Are Spoken

Leader's Notes

MY GRACE IS SUFFICIENT FOR YOU. (2 COR 12:9)

Leading a Bible discussion can be an enjoyable and rewarding experience. But it can also be *scary*—especially if you've never done it before. If this is your feeling, you're in good company. When God asked Moses to lead the Israelites out of Egypt, he replied, "O LORD, please send someone else to do it" (Ex 4:13). It was the same with Solomon, Jeremiah and Timothy, but God helped these people in spite of their weaknesses, and he will help you as well.

You don't need to be an expert on the Bible or a trained teacher to lead a Bible discussion. The idea behind these inductive studies is that the leader guides group members to discover for themselves what the Bible has to say. This method of learning will allow group members to remember much more of what is said than a lecture would.

These studies are designed to be led easily. As a matter of fact, the flow of questions through the passage from observation to interpretation to application is so natural that you may feel that the studies lead themselves. This study guide is also flexible. You can use it with a variety of groups—student, professional, neighborhood or church groups. Each study takes forty-five to sixty minutes in a group setting.

There are some important facts to know about group dynamics and encouraging discussion. The suggestions listed below should enable you to effectively and enjoyably fulfill your role as leader.

Preparing for the Study

1. Ask God to help you understand and apply the passage in your own life. Unless this happens, you will not be prepared to lead others. Pray too for the various members of the group. Ask God to open your hearts to the message of his Word and motivate you to action.

2. Read the introduction to the entire guide to get an overview of the entire book and the issues which will be explored.

3. As you begin each study, read and reread the assigned Bible passage to familiarize yourself with it.

4. This study guide is based on the New International Version of the Bible. It will help you and the group if you use this translation as the basis for your study and discussion.

5. Carefully work through each question in the study. Spend time in meditation and reflection as you consider how to respond.

6. Write your thoughts and responses in the space provided in the study guide. This will help you to express your understanding of the passage clearly.

7. It might help to have a Bible dictionary handy. Use it to look up any unfamiliar words, names or places. (For additional help on how to study a passage, see chapter five of *How to Lead a LifeGuide Bible Study,* InterVarsity Press.)

8. Consider how you can apply the Scripture to your life. Remember that the group will follow your lead in responding to the studies. They will not go any deeper than you do.

9. Once you have finished your own study of the passage, familiarize yourself with the leader's notes for the study you are leading. These are designed to help you in several ways. First, they tell you the purpose the study guide author had in mind when writing the study. Take time to think through how the study questions work together to accomplish that purpose. Second, the notes provide you with additional background information or suggestions on group dynamics for various questions. This information can be useful when people have difficulty understanding or answering a question. Third, the leader's notes can alert you to potential problems you may encounter during the study.

10. If you wish to remind yourself of anything mentioned in the leader's notes, make a note to yourself below that question in the study.

Leading the Study

1. Begin the study on time. Open with prayer, asking God to help the group to understand and apply the passage.

2. Be sure that everyone in your group has a study guide. Encourage the group to prepare beforehand for each discussion by reading the introduction to the guide and by working through the questions in the study.

3. At the beginning of your first time together, explain that these studies are meant to be discussions, not lectures. Encourage the members of the group to participate. However, do not put pressure on those who may be hesitant to speak during the first few sessions. You may want to suggest the following guidelines to your group.

☐ Stick to the topic being discussed.

☐ Your responses should be based on the verses which are the focus of the discussion and not on outside authorities such as commentaries or speakers.

☐ These studies focus on a particular passage of Scripture. Only rarely should you refer to other portions of the Bible. This allows for everyone to participate in in-depth study on equal ground.

☐ Anything said in the group is considered confidential and will not be discussed outside the group unless specific permission is given to do so.

☐ We will listen attentively to each other and provide time for each person present to talk.

☐ We will pray for each other.

4. Have a group member read the introduction at the beginning of the discussion.

5. Every session begins with a group discussion question. The question or activity is meant to be used before the passage is read. The question introduces the theme of the study and encourages group members to begin to open up. Encourage as many members as possible to participate, and be ready to get the discussion going with your own response.

This section is designed to reveal where our thoughts or feelings need to be transformed by Scripture. That is why it is especially important not to read the passage before the discussion question is asked. The passage will tend to color the honest reactions people would otherwise give because they are, of course, supposed to think the way the Bible does.

You may want to supplement the group discussion question with an ice-breaker to help people to get comfortable. See the community section of *Small Group Idea Book* for more ideas.

You also might want to use the personal reflection question with your group. Either allow a time of silence for people to respond individually or discuss it together.

6. Have a group member (or members if the passage is long) read aloud the passage to be studied. Then give people several minutes to read the passage again silently so that they can take it all in.

7. Question 1 will generally be an overview question designed to briefly survey the passage. Encourage the group to look at the whole passage, but try to avoid getting sidetracked by questions or issues that will be addressed later in the study.

8. As you ask the questions, keep in mind that they are designed to be used just as they are written. You may simply read them aloud. Or you may prefer to express them in your own words.

There may be times when it is appropriate to deviate from the study guide.

For example, a question may have already been answered. If so, move on to the next question. Or someone may raise an important question not covered in the guide. Take time to discuss it, but try to keep the group from going off on tangents.

9. Avoid answering your own questions. If necessary, repeat or rephrase them until they are clearly understood. Or point out something you read in the leader's notes to clarify the context or meaning. An eager group quickly becomes passive and silent if they think the leader will do most of the talking.

10. Don't be afraid of silence. People may need time to think about the question before formulating their answers.

11. Don't be content with just one answer. Ask, "What do the rest of you think?" or "Anything else?" until several people have given answers to the question.

12. Acknowledge all contributions. Try to be affirming whenever possible. Never reject an answer. If it is clearly off-base, ask, "Which verse led you to that conclusion?" or again, "What do the rest of you think?"

13. Don't expect every answer to be addressed to you, even though this will probably happen at first. As group members become more at ease, they will begin to truly interact with each other. This is one sign of healthy discussion.

14. Don't be afraid of controversy. It can be very stimulating. If you don't resolve an issue completely, don't be frustrated. Move on and keep it in mind for later. A subsequent study may solve the problem.

15. Periodically summarize what the group has said about the passage. This helps to draw together the various ideas mentioned and gives continuity to the study. But don't preach.

16. At the end of the Bible discussion you may want to allow group members a time of quiet to work on an idea under "Now or Later." Then discuss what you experienced. Or you may want to encourage group members to work on these ideas between meetings. Give an opportunity during the session for people to talk about what they are learning.

17. Conclude your time together with conversational prayer, adapting the prayer suggestion at the end of the study to your group. Ask for God's help in following through on the commitments you've made.

18. End on time.

Many more suggestions and helps are found in *How to Lead a LifeGuide Bible Study.*

Components of Small Groups

A healthy small group should do more than study the Bible. There are four components to consider as you structure your time together.

Nurture. Small groups help us to grow in our knowledge and love of God. Bible study is the key to making this happen and is the foundation of your small group.

Community. Small groups are a great place to develop deep friendships with other Christians. Allow time for informal interaction before and after each study. Plan activities and games that will help you get to know each other. Spend time having fun together—going on a picnic or cooking dinner together.

Worship and prayer. Your study will be enhanced by spending time praising God together in prayer or song. Pray for each other's needs—and keep track of how God is answering prayer in your group. Ask God to help you to apply what you are learning in your study.

Outreach. Reaching out to others can be a practical way of applying what you are learning, and it will keep your group from becoming self-focused. Host a series of evangelistic discussions for your friends or neighbors. Clean up the yard of an elderly friend. Serve at a soup kitchen together, or spend a day working on a Habitat house.

Many more suggestions and helps in each of these areas are found in *Small Group Idea Book.* Information on building a small group can be found in *Small Group Leaders' Handbook* and *The Big Book on Small Groups* (both from Inter-Varsity Press). Reading through one of these books would be worth your time.

Study 1. Good Shepherd. John 10:1-18.
Purpose: To follow Christ with increasing trust.
Question 1. "The thief (in the context, unfaithful leaders; cf. v. 5) acts for his own good, not that of the flock (hungry thieves might steal sheep for food); a shepherd risks his life to protect his flock from animals and thieves. . . . A hired helper was not responsible for attacks from wild animals (Ex 22:13) and worked for pay, not because the sheep were his own. Religious leaders who let God's sheep be scattered are not his true agents or representatives, because they are not concerned with what concerns him" (Craig S. Keener, *The IVP Bible Background Commentary: New Testament* [Downers Grove, Ill.: InterVarsity Press, 1993], p. 290).
Question 3. "The characteristic of a true shepherd is that he not only recognizes his sheep but calls them by name and leads them out to pasture (4). Clearly no such personal relationship could exist between strangers and the sheep (5)" (Gordon J. Wenham, J. Alec Motyer, Donald A. Carson and R. T. France, eds., *New Bible Commentary: 21st Century Edition* [Downers Grove, Ill.: InterVarsity Press, 1994], p. 1046).

Question 5. "Several scholars have cited a modern example of shepherds sleeping across the gateway to serve both as shepherd and door, but Jesus probably alternates between images simply because he fulfills more than one role; like God in the Old Testament, he is Israel's shepherd, but he is also the way to the Father" (*IVP Bible Background Commentary: NT,* p. 290).

Question 9. The Good Shepherd is intimate with the Father, and he offers his followers the same intimacy with himself (vv. 14-15). His concern goes beyond his immediate flock; he will go to others far away and gather them in also (v. 16). Verse 17 seems to say that the Father's love is dependent on the Son laying down his life, but this would be inconsistent with the rest of the Gospel of John. Jesus claimed perfect oneness with the Father (Jn 10:30). He said, "The Father loves the Son and shows him all he does" (Jn 5:20), confirming the words of John the Baptist: "The Father loves the Son and has placed everything in his hands" (Jn 3:35). The night before he was crucified, Jesus told his disciples, "As the Father has loved me, so have I loved you" (Jn 15:9). Nothing can destroy the Father's love for the Son. No one forces the Good Shepherd to lay down his life; he gives it freely and can take it up again (v. 18).

Study 2. Lamb of God. Revelation 5:6-14.
Purpose: To have a renewed sense of the enormity of Christ's sacrifice for sin.
General note. The apostle John, in exile on the island of Patmos, had an extended vision of heaven. He first saw the triumphant Christ, who gave him messages for seven ancient churches (Rev 1—3). John was then summoned to heaven, where he saw a throne with an indescribable Person sitting on it surrounded by worshipers (Rev 4). The One on the throne held in his right hand a scroll that no one was worthy to open (Rev 5:1-5). The Scripture for today's study begins at that point. While some group members may be eager to discuss different views of prophecy and the end times, remember that the overall theme of this study guide is *scriptural images of Jesus Christ*—in this case, a Lamb who has been killed but is alive. Keep your study and your group members focused on the Lamb.

Question 1. The Lion of Judah refers to the promised ruler of Genesis 49:9-10. While the lion was a symbol of power, the helpless lamb was quite the opposite. Isaiah prophesied of the Messiah, "he was led like a lamb to the slaughter, and as a sheep before her shearers is silent, so he did not open his mouth" (Is 53:7). Lambs were used for various Old Testament sacrifices. John the Baptist identified Jesus as the ultimate sacrifice, "the Lamb of God, who takes away the sin of the world" (Jn 1:29).

Question 2. The Lamb has triumphed over death (has been slain but is alive), commands the place of God (stands in the center of the throne), possesses great power and knowledge (has seven horns and seven eyes) and is uniquely worthy (takes from God's right hand the scroll that no one else can open).

Question 3. The worshipers sing a new song because the Lamb has ushered in a new reality. He has accomplished what no one else could accomplish. By his death he purchased the lives of people all over the world, and he has made them into God's servants who will reign on Earth. Not only human beings but all the angels and all creation worship him and will continue to worship him forever.

Question 5. The Lamb has purchased human beings from "every tribe and language and people and nation" (v. 9). All believers are united in Christ regardless of nationality or race or ethnic identity. He gave himself for all.

Question 7. This Lamb that John sees in his vision is regal and majestic. He has infinite authority, knowledge and power. He accepts the worship that only God deserves.

Study 3. Suffering Servant. Isaiah 52:13—53:6.
Purpose: To take Christ as our example of sacrificial service.

Question 1. Although verse 13 promises that the servant will be "raised and lifted up and highly exalted," the rest of the passage portrays him as the opposite. He is unattractive, despised, rejected, afflicted, crushed and punished for others' sins although he is innocent. On this side of Christ's resurrection we know that he is now exalted, but at his crucifixion he appeared to be the most beaten down of humanity.

Question 3. "For *sprinkle*, the RSV's 'startle' (supported by the LXX [Septuagint]) makes a good opening to the sequence, startled—silenced—convinced. But *sprinkle* (AV, RV), which is grammatically suspect but not indefensible, suits the context well with its implications of sacrificial cleansing (*cf.* 1 Pet. 1:2)" (*New Bible Commentary,* p. 662).

Question 4. "The suffering servant will grow up 'like a root out of dry ground' (Is 53:2 NRSV). While this could be taken as a blessing—plant life emerging from arid soil—it is most likely meant to portray the opposite. The context speaks of rejection and isolation, pointing to a meager plant struggling for survival in a land of sparse vegetation" (Leland Ryken, James C. Wilhoit, Tremper Longman III, eds., *Dictionary of Biblical Imagery* [Downers Grove, Ill.: InterVarsity Press, 1998], p. 826).

Question 6. The final phrase of verse 6 reveals the answer: "The Lord has laid on him the iniquity of us all." God takes away our punishment for sin and places it on the innocent servant. God does this not because he hates the servant but because he loves us, and through his mercy we enjoy peace and healing (v. 5).

Question 7. People assume that God punishes the servant for his own wrongdoing. When Jesus was crucified, onlookers mocked him because God did not come to rescue him (Mt 27:39-44). Yet God's purposes in the crucifixion were for the good of the onlookers and all humanity. Jesus would be exalted after he had paid the penalty for sin.

Study 4. Branch. Isaiah 11:1-9.

Purpose: To see the faithfulness of God in keeping his promise of a Messiah.

Question 1. The Branch will judge by the standard of righteousness rather than by outward appearance. He will bring justice to the poor, in contrast to the unfairness they normally receive. He will reconcile former enemies, even those that seem irreconcilable. He will do away with danger and harm.

Question 3. "Within the visions of a coming golden age, the image of the branch receives special focus as a symbol of the Messiah. Thus 'there shall come forth a shoot from the stump of Jesse, and a branch shall grow out of his roots' (Is 11:1 RSV)" (*Dictionary of Biblical Imagery,* p. 116).

Question 5. Most earthly rulers lack the attributes of verse 2, except for *power,* and they usually exert their power to dominate others. In contrast to verses 3-4, earthly rulers tend to judge by appearances, neglect the poor and acquit the wicked. They surround themselves with the belt of self-preservation rather than righteousness and faithfulness (v. 5).

Question 6. The harmonious pairings are startling and radical: wolf and lamb; leopard and goat; calf, lion, yearling (calf) and little child; cow and bear; lion and ox (the lion will eat like the ox); infant and cobra; and young child and viper. In nature as it exists today, we would never find these pairs or groups living together in harmony and safety. Something earth-changing must happen to make such a vision possible.

Question 8. "In this idyllic scene the title 'Prince of Peace' (9:6) is perfectly unfolded. Significantly, peace is hard-won; it follows judgment (*cf.* v 4b) and springs from righteousness (*cf.* v 5), true to the sequence expounded in 32:17. Its heart, however, is the relationship expressed as *the knowledge of the* LORD" (*New Bible Commentary,* p. 640).

Study 5. True Vine. John 15:1-8.

Purpose: To increase in spiritual fruit as we cling to Christ.

Question 1. "Drawing in minute ways on actual practices of pruning, Jesus pictures the nature of Christian growth, an important part of which is that

God prunes every branch that bears fruit, 'that it may bear more fruit' (Jn 15:2). Far from being an image of punishment, pruning signifies nurture, growth and fruitfulness" (*Dictionary of Biblical Imagery*, p. 684).

Question 3. The answer to this question includes both the botanical relationship of vine to branches and the metaphorical relationship of Christ to his followers. "Speaking to the disciples, Jesus proclaims, 'I am the vine; you are the branches' (Jn 15:5 NIV). By identifying himself as the vine he claims that participation in the kingdom is possible only for those who 'remain in' him. Those disciples who do will bear much fruit" (*Dictionary of Biblical Imagery*, p. 684).

Question 4. "Jesus was the *true vine* in the sense of being genuine as compared with Israel which had not acted in harmony with its calling. Jesus was the reality of which Israel was but the type" (*New Bible Commentary*, p. 1055).

Question 5. "Pruning is the most important operation for maintaining the fruitfulness of the vine. A completely fruitless branch is not worthy of its place in the vine and has to be removed, whereas weak branches can be strengthened by being pruned. Among the disciples Judas was removed while the others had to undergo 'pruning' experiences before producing fruit after Pentecost" (*New Bible Commentary*, p. 1055).

Question 7. Many things can contribute to a fruitful Christian life. Perhaps the most important factors are set forth by Paul in Galatians 5:16-25.

Question 8. "Just as the Father has loved Jesus, so Jesus has loved his disciples, and they are to abide in his love (15:9). Just as Jesus has remained in his Father's love by obeying his commands, . . . so the disciples are to abide in Jesus' love by obeying his commands (15:10). And as they abide in him, Jesus will convey his life to them, even as a vine gives life to its branches (15:4-6). His life will manifest itself in their lives as they bear fruit, even as his works were the work of his Father. Apart from him the disciples can do nothing, just as Jesus could do nothing apart from the Father (5:19, 30)" (W. L. Kynes, "Abiding," in *Dictionary of Jesus and the Gospels*, ed. Joel B. Green and Scot McKnight [Downers Grove, Ill.: InterVarsity Press, 1992], p. 2).

Question 10. If God is the source of all good, then any good works done on this earth must ultimately come from him, whether the doers recognize God or not. Good works done with no thought of God are beneficial to those who receive them, but they accomplish nothing of eternal significance. The apostle Paul counted his worldly righteousness as "rubbish," which literally means either *dung* or *leftovers from a feast* (Phil 3:8). The prophet Isaiah likened his people's righteous acts to filthy rags (Is 64:6). Even good works done in the name of Christ cannot buy forgiveness or bring us to heaven; salvation is "not by works, so that no one can boast" (Eph 2:9).

Question 12. "Remaining in the vine is closely linked with prayer. Those close enough to the vine will not wish to ask anything not in line with the vine himself" (*New Bible Commentary,* p. 1055).

Study 6. Light of the World. John 1:1-9.
Purpose: To see ourselves and others in the light of Christ.
Question 3. "The designation of Jesus as 'God' occurs once more, in John 20:28, when the risen Jesus is confessed as 'Lord and God.' Elsewhere, Jesus is accused of 'making himself equal to God' (5:18) and 'making himself God' (10:33)" (Marianne Meye Thompson, in *Dictionary of Jesus and the Gospels,* pp. 376-77).
Questions 4-5. "There . . . is an illumination which comes to everyone generally and would seem to refer to the light of conscience and reason. In v 5, however, the focus falls on the environment which is described as *darkness.* The light, which is closely linked with the Word, must be regarded as personal. It must mean the spiritual enlightenment which humankind has received exclusively through the coming of the Word. The following statement, *but the darkness has not understood it,* could be translated as 'has not overcome it.' Both interpretations express a truth, and both are illustrated in the body of the gospel. But the former fits the context better, especially in the light of vs 10-11" (*New Bible Commentary,* p. 1025).
Question 6. "Not only is it expressly denied that John himself was the light, but his function as witness to the light is twice affirmed (7-8). The purpose, *so that through him all men might believe,* expresses the function of all true Christian witness, from that day to this" (*New Bible Commentary,* p. 1025).
Question 7. Ask group members to think of anything that "dazzles" but which leads to destruction. While the uses of *light* in Scripture overwhelmingly refer to God, Paul cautioned that "Satan himself masquerades as an angel of light" (2 Cor 11:14).
Question 8. Scripture affirms that there is a knowledge of the truth that God gives to every person, although people do not obey it. See Romans 1:18-22.

Study 7. Bridegroom. Ephesians 5:25-33.
Purpose: To be wholly devoted to Christ, who gave himself for us.
Question 1. This passage from Ephesians is potentially volatile because of the well-known admonition that precedes it, that wives should submit to their husbands as to the Lord (vv. 22-24). It is vital to keep the discussion focused on the passage at hand and on Paul's application of the husband-wife relationship to Christ and the church.

Question 3. Christ gave himself up for the church, not only in service but by offering his own life as the final sufficient sacrifice for her sin (v. 25). *The church* here in Ephesians is not a building or a particular denomination but *all Christians.* The Greek word is *ekklesia,* literally "the called out," also used of an assembly of people. The word *church* has the same meaning throughout the New Testament except where it refers to a particular local group of Christian believers, such as the seven churches in Revelation 2—3, and even there the word refers to people rather than buildings.

"After stressing the mutuality of submission (Eph 5:21), Paul, in Ephesians 5:23, calls the husband head of the wife 'as Christ is head of the church, himself Savior of the body.' The extended passage stresses the concern of Christ, the bridegroom, for the full development of his bride, the church; and husbands are called to a similar concern. As Christ the head brought growth and empowerment to the body of believers (Eph 4:15; Col 2:10), so the husband should be the enabler of the wife for personal growth and empowerment in a society that afforded her few opportunities" (Gerald F. Hawthorne, Ralph P. Martin, Daniel G. Reid, eds., *Dictionary of Paul and His Letters* [Downers Grove, Ill.: InterVarsity Press, 1993], p. 377).

Question 4. The "washing" of verse 26 "probably alludes figuratively to the bride's prenuptial washing (of course, washing was natural before any occasion on which one wished to impress another positively). After this washing the bride was perfumed, anointed and arrayed in wedding clothes. The betrothal ceremony in Judaism also came to be called 'the sanctification of the bride,' setting her apart for her husband. The 'word' naturally refers to the saving gospel of Christ (1:13)" (*IVP Bible Background Commentary: NT,* p. 552).

Paul's description of Christ presented with a flawless bride (v. 27) has been distorted to mean "the restoration of the church"—the idea that before Christ returns, genuine Christians will be called out of the organizational church to become the purified bride of Christ on earth, ready to meet the bridegroom. The picture in Ephesians 5, consistent with the rest of the New Testament, is that Christ's sacrifice cancels our debt of sin so that we stand guiltless before God (Eph 1:7-8; 2:8-9). We are "holy and blameless" not because we have left a corrupt organization, but because Christ has paid for our wrongs.

Of the sacrificial love of Christ in Ephesians, J. I. Packer wrote:

> Christ's love was *free,* not elicited by any goodness in us (2:1-5); it was *eternal,* being one with the choice of sinners to save which the father made "before the creation of the world" (1:4); it was *unreserved,* for it led him down to the depths of humiliation and, indeed, of hell itself on Calvary; and it was *sovereign,* for it has achieved its object—the final glory of

the redeemed, their perfect holiness and happiness in the fruition of his love (5:26-27), is now guaranteed and assured (1:14; 2:7-10; 4:11-16; 4:30). Dwell on these things, Paul urges, if you would catch a sight, however dim, of the greatness and the glory of divine love." (J. I. Packer, *Knowing God* [Downers Grove, Ill.: InterVarsity Press, 1993], p. 197)

Question 7. Encourage group members to particularly recall times they have gone to the Lord with urgent prayer or have had to trust him when all circumstances indicated otherwise. Here is a good time to remind group members that the Lord is faithful to us and that he remains close to us even if we do not sense his immediate presence.

Study 8. Head of the Church. Colossians 1:15-20.
Purpose: To submit to Christ as the all-sufficient Lord of the church.

Question 4. "As an image of the relationship of Christ and the church, Paul adopts the symbolism of head in connection to the body (Col 1:18; 2:19; Eph 4:15; 5:23). He appears to rely on a widespread and common conception . . . that there is a twofold sense of leadership and source of provision denoted by the head when it is used in association with the body. Thus when Paul speaks of Christ as the head, he implies that he not only provides leadership to the church but that he nourishes the body by supplying whatever it needs for its ongoing growth and development (see esp. Col 2:19; Eph 5:23)" (*Dictionary of Biblical Imagery,* p. 368).

Question 5. It would be intriguing to ask how various aspects of your own local church would be different if Christ were allowed to have his way absolutely in each: finances, building plans, committees, worship, hiring of staff and so forth. However, Paul's point here is not that we should allow Christ to rule in the decisions of the church; rather, Paul states that Christ *is* Head of the church, whether we like it or not and whether we acknowledge it or not. Outside of Christ the church may have physical life but can have no spiritual life.

Question 6. Jesus was both fully human and fully God. Paul uses the same Greek word translated "fullness" a few lines later in Colossians 2:9: "For in Christ all the fullness of the Deity lives in bodily form." Jesus was not partly God or a temporary container for God. He was (and is) God himself.

Question 7. Christ's death on the cross brings peace between a holy God and sinful humanity. We cannot understand or appreciate his reconciliation until we admit that we are rebels who are alienated from God. We become reconciled not because we bring the right peace terms to the table but because Jesus has paid for the sin of our rebellion.

Question 10. Any time the church depends on Christ *plus* something else, it denies the supremacy of its Head. The false teachers in Colossae insisted that believers needed Christ *plus* a secret system of knowledge. Other dangerous dependencies are Christ plus good works, Christ plus ritual, Christ plus self-discipline, and Christ plus human philosophies.

Study 9. Bread of Life. John 6:25-51.
Purpose: To rely on Jesus for everything we need, physically and spiritually.
Question 1. "In biblical times bread was the staple food, a synonym for food itself and even the symbol for that which in any way might sustain physical life (Deut 8:3). Paradoxically, the ordinariness of bread is the basis of its extraordinary importance in the Gospels. There was little change in the way it was made down to the time of Jesus. Bread was made from the flour of ground wheat or barley. The flour was mixed with salt and water and the dough baked in an oven or on a metal griddle in a leavened or unleavened state. The loaves were of varying shapes and sizes, sometimes flat and round or in the shape of a modern rectangular loaf. The barley loaves (Jn 6:9) were of a lesser quality and were the food of the poor" (*Dictionary of Jesus and the Gospels*, p. 83).
Question 2. "The Bible's most striking metaphorical use of bread appears in John 6. Here Jesus declares that he is 'the bread of life' (v. 35; cf. vv. 33, 41, 48, 51). The image is appropriate because John 6 brings together all the major biblical themes associated with bread. The bread from heaven is said to be a gift from above—'my Father gives you the true bread from heaven' (v. 32). Jesus' multiplication of loaves and fish recalls Elisha's similar miracle (2 Kings 4:42-44) and is explicitly compared with the provision of manna in the wilderness (vv. 31-34, 49-51). The bread that is Jesus gives life in the present (vv. 35, 47) but also means eternal life (vv. 27, 40). Finally, Jesus associates himself as the true bread with the Eucharist: 'Unless you eat the flesh of the Son of man and drink his blood, you have no life in you' (v. 53)" (*Dictionary of Biblical Imagery*, p. 118).
Question 3. "The dialogue between Jesus and the crowd plays on the term *work*; Judaism stressed righteous works, but Jesus singles out one work: faith in him (Jewish teachers praised Abraham's 'work' of faith in God, but Jesus' demand is more specific). They then demand from Jesus a 'work,' which now means a sign (v. 30), as it sometimes does in Jewish literature" (*IVP Bible Background Commentary: NT*, p. 279).
Question 5. The "manna in the desert" (v. 31) or "bread from heaven" (vv. 31-32) was the miraculous food, which God provided for the Israelites during their journey from Egypt to Canaan (Exodus 16).
"This passage [vv. 30-59] is a regular Jewish midrash, or homily, on Exodus 16:15 and Psalm 78:24, which Jesus quotes in John 6:31. Jesus para-

phrases, explains and expounds in a manner characteristic of ancient Jewish teachers, yet his hearers fail to understand him. Ancient teachers sometimes made their lectures hard to understand to sort out genuine followers from the masses" (*IVP Bible Background Commentary: NT,* pp. 279-80).

Question 8. "V 35 records the first of the great 'I am' sayings of Jesus, and the following verses (35-51) are an expanded commentary on it. It is a direct response to the people's demand for bread, for it was necessary for them to understand that Jesus was speaking of spiritual not physical food. The meaning of the phrase *bread of life* is bread which gives life, but such bread is available only to those who believe in Jesus, a condition which the hearers had not fulfilled (36). If Jesus' mission depended on the faith of the people, does this suggest a failure? V 37 gives the answer. The final result is in the Father's hands. *Whoever comes* shows an emphasis on the individual response. The emphatic negative statement *I will never drive away* is to be understood as an assurance that Jesus will preserve them. There is no possibility of any disagreement between the Father and the Son, as vs 38-39 show. What the Father gives the Son will receive—*I shall lose none.* Note that the *all* in v 39 is neuter (as in v 37) and sums up everything given by the Father to the Son. The two references to the *last day* (40) show that Jesus was thinking ahead to the end of the age, when all will be consummated" (*New Bible Commentary,* p. 1038).

Question 9. "There are unmistakable references to the coming Last Supper in the narrative; the following verses (6:52-57) make this clear. But Jesus is also referring to his sacrificial death, particularly in 6:51. The mention of manna as an ordinary food is intended to show the superiority of Jesus to the law" (J. F. Ross, "Bread," in *Interpreter's Dictionary of the Bible,* ed. George A. Buttrick, vol. 1 [Nashville: Abingdon Press, 1962], p. 463).

Question 11. The standard answers that come to mind are prayer, Bible study, church attendance and fellowship with other believers. Those are all important and helpful, and Christians should habitually practice them all. But we easily fall into dependence on our own works and imagine that it's up to us to nourish ourselves by what we do. Jesus himself is the bread we require for life. He nourishes us and meets all our needs with his own sufficiency. Christians hold varying convictions about the role of Communion in our nourishment on the bread of life. Feel free to compare group members' ideas, but keep Christ and not Communion central to the discussion.

Study 10. Cornerstone. 1 Peter 2:4-8.
Purpose: To build our lives on the sure foundation of Christ.
Question 1. "The church takes its alignment from him [Christ] as a building

takes its alignment from the cornerstone (Eph. 2:20-21). It derives its unity and growth from him (Eph. 2:19-22; 4:15-16). The life of the church is maintained by its vital union with him (Rom. 6:1-4; Eph. 2:21-22; 4:15-16, and by contrast, Col. 2:19) and exists only insofar as it is 'in him'. The person and work of Christ, then, are at the heart of the NT view of the *ekklesia* [church]" (T. Desmond Alexander and Brian S. Rosner, eds., *New Dictionary of Biblical Theology* [Downers Grove, Ill.: InterVarsity Press, 2000], p. 408].

Question 3. We may build Christ a physical house (a place of worship), but we cannot build his spiritual house. Christ himself builds us into his own spiritual house of which he is the vital cornerstone. Our part is to come to him (v. 4) and trust in him (v. 6).

Question 5. "God's future purpose, revealed to Isaiah, was to lay in Zion 'a foundation stone, a tested stone, a precious cornerstone, a sure foundation' (Is 28:16 NRSV) and to use builders of justice and righteousness. The cornerstone here is part of the foundation, whereas in other contexts it could be the key top stone (Zech 4:7, 9). The NT makes use of both senses. The top stone of an arch or pediment proved that the architect's instruction had been carried out and so exactly illustrated the work of Christ, the 'living stone' (1 Pet 2:4). Peter also quotes Psalm 118:22: 'The stone that the builders rejected has become the very head of the corner' (1 Pet 2:7 NRSV) together with Isaiah 8:14. These references were linked by the first Christians because they point to Jesus as the Messiah foretold in the Scriptures (cf. Acts 4:11): though their Messiah had caused division and was rejected by many, this had been predicted. Jesus himself was the source of this application of Psalm 118:22, to which he added a reference to the stone of Daniel 2:34: 'Everyone who falls on that stone will be broken to pieces; and it will crush anyone on whom it falls' (Lk 20:17-18). This dreadful picture of judgment from the lips of Jesus is found only in the Gospels" (*Dictionary of Biblical Imagery*, pp. 815-16).

Question 6. The word *stumble* occurs twice in verse 8. It is the same word used for physical stumbling in John 11:9-10. The righteousness which Christ offers us is contrary to our natural drive to try to work our way to God. The person who is busy pursuing self-justification trips and falls over the radical good news of Christ.

Dale and Sandy Larsen are freelance writers in Greenville, Illinois. Together they have written more than thirty books and Bible studies, including six other LifeGuide® Bible Studies and Jonathan Edwards, Teresa of Ávila and Dietrich Bonhoeffer in the Christian Classics Series.

  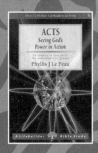 
  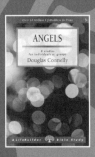